Women Building The World, A Poetic International Women's Day Collection

Kimberly Burnham, Editor

Thuthukani Ndlovu, Collection Curator

The Poets

Charlotte Addison

Kimberly Burnham

Sasha Leigh Coutinho

Ruth Ekong

Amina Hussain El-Yakub

Debbie Johnson

Usha Krishnamurthy

Alicja Maria Kuberska

Vimbai Josephine Lole

Cathrine Chidawanyika Makuvise

Chiwawa Fungai Manana

Tanyaradzwa Masaire

Kearoma Desiree Mosata

Xolani Msimango

Cheryl Zvikomborero Musimwa

Patience Osei Bonsu

Sandhya Padmanabhan

Toiwa Petronella

Nyakallo Posholi

Michelle L. Schmid

Linda Simone

Itzela Sosa

Rutendo Matewu Tigere

Latha Y

Ruth Yacim

Women Building The World, A Poetic International Women's Day Collection ©2016

Kimberly Burnham, Editor
Thuthukani Ndlovu, Collection Curator

Creating Calm Network, Publisher
Cover Art Designed by Thuthukani Ndlovu

ISBN: 978-1-937207-18-2

Table of Contents

3

4

5

"You may not always have a comfortable life and you will not always be able to solve all of the world's problems at once but don't ever underestimate the importance you can have because history has shown us that courage can be contagious and hope can take on a life of its own."
— Michelle Obama

"In Nigeria, along with its West African neighbor Ghana, women are now starting businesses in greater numbers than men."
— Gayle Tzemach Lemmon

"Change happens by listening and then starting a dialogue with the people who are doing something you don't believe is right."
— Jane Goodall

"When we do the best we can, we never know what miracle is wrought in our life, or in the life of another."
—Helen Keller

Introduction

In your hands is a collection of poems from 25 poets, women from around the world. Some of the poems are stunningly beautiful, some inspiring or thought provoking. They are the words of women's experience, of our lives, and for what we yearn for ourselves, our families, and our communities. As you may know, English language spelling varies from country to country and so the editorial choice was made to leave the spelling the way the poet wrote it, honoring our diversity even in the use of language.

Some of the women are old and some are young but we see the bond we have with each other. We use poetry to cross the boundaries and sometimes the walls that divide us to find common ground. Beyond making the world a better place, our voices help build the world. Please enjoy the run of emotions that flow in these pages. And contact the individual poets to share in more of their world building work.

Each poem, writing style, experience, or emotion will appeal to different people. This is the beauty of an anthology. It is a rich lush world created in the pages of one book, built in this case by many women.

My personal favorites include "In a Different World" by Rutendo Matewu, because I can relate to her experience. It begins ... "If I could turn back the hands of time..." What would you do differently if you could turn back the hands of time?

Another of my favorite poems in this collection is 'From A Mother's Lips.' Chiwawa Fungai Manana describes mixed feelings about the birth of her daughter but she is unequivocal in the love she has for her. While I have not given birth, children who I love have come into my life and Chiwawa's poem shines a light on the complicated relationship women have with their children and how messy and wonderful it can be at the same time.

I hope that you enjoy these and all of the poems.

— Kimberly (Nerve Whisperer) Burnham, Spokane, WA, USA

"Optimism is the faith that leads to achievement."
— Helen Keller

A Word From the Curator

Greetings fellow readers and thank you for taking the time to open this book. This is the third book for this year, and this time around I decided to dedicate the book to International Women's Day (March 8). Unlike the first two books: "From the Motherland" and "All About Love," this book only features female poets from around the world. I wanted to give women the platform to showcase their poetry, therefore creating a book that will hopefully be a source of inspiration, wisdom, and information for women around the world. This does not mean the book is not for men (I actually learned a lot from it), for I believe men of different ages can also learn something from the poems gathered here.

I can guarantee you that this book will provide you with an experience that will satisfy your mind, heart, and spirit, so without further ado, I hope you enjoy this amazing collection of poetry.

—Thuthukani Ndlovu, Collection Curator, Bloemfontein, South Africa

She

If it took God an hour to mould a man,
It must have taken him twice to form a she
A she, a master piece full of intricacies
Best hanged in the Louvre to shine and blind
The world of PHD'S—Pull her down

She is home—home to many lovers and
grandchildren,
Who fetch wisdom from her Well and suck the milk
From her kitchen
Even the homeless make merry outside her gate
And dance to the tune of delicacies on her table
She balances a pot of intelligence on her head
And makes Einstein bow at her feet with gladness
She is a womb that juggles the worst
And births nations from shackled dreams
She wipes the darkness with her tears
And make holes of escape in walls
Walls built to cave her in
She salutes her sisters from another mother
And bears them with hefty arms
She loves intense, it strangles her heart
Yet she loves the same
She is a whirl wind that can't be tamed

And a wound to the chauvinist's ego
She burns the teeth that bites her tongue
She is unbridled fire!
She is a WOMAN!

— Charlotte Addison, Ghana

"A woman with a voice is by definition a strong woman. But the search to find that voice can be remarkably difficult."
— Melinda Gates

"Women are vital beings and for that matter must be upheld. They are complementary beings, even at the time of creation. Women can play more influential roles in society when they take up positions even those reserved for men, and dare to do more, ignoring the intimidations and obstacles that may come her way. By so doing, she builds up her confidence and maturity levels, making her powerful."
—Patience (Nana Ama) Osei Bonsu, Ghana

Imprints

Should I make a bed of your Poetry
or hold it tight close to my heart.

Should it leave its imprint on my mind,
or print it on my body.

All in all let me hold it so close
that the scribbles & scratches

Composed so lovingly should
leave its tell tale marks
both on my body and soul.

So let me make a bed of
your poetry and hold it
close to my heart
and let it sing its
sweet soulful music
to mingle our Body & Soul.

— Usha Krishnamurthy, India

Wo(rld)man

To her that was birthed by rain drops that penetrated
dust
moulded by fire
kept alive by air
to her that glows like the sun
with eyes that reflect the moonlight and a twinkling
tongue
for her mountains shrink from her ungloated strength
for she crashes rocks, stabs knives and ignites sparks
with her bare hand

When she speaks sunflowers blossom in the night
time

She cries to fill the river until it flows to fill the
drought lines to nourish the soil.

She plants seeds that are ripped by her Harsh feet that
walk through thorns to feed her children

For her the womb bows in honour, for it is carried
graciously by a soul that bears great nations

She is the globe that shines the heavens, the light

In her fullness she carries and sustains life.

The walking flower that stands on the world's peak;
She stands on her own peak
She is the world.

— Nyakallo (Azanian_Nile_Lily) Posholi, South Africa

"If you want something said, ask a man; If you want something done, ask a woman."
—Margaret Thatcher

"A woman's heart is the most powerful weapon she wields. A woman who understands the tears, joys and strength of her heart can win the whole world. A woman's heart is capable of healing and killing. The aura of strength and energy around a woman is derived from her heart. In the heart of woman lays her Power."
—Charlotte Addison, Ghana

Things My Mother Taught Me

My mother never taught me how to leave.
She never sat me down and laid it down
that when push came to shove,
I should save my soul
and run.

She never taught me to run
when I saw that there was no room
for my over loving heart.
When my soul tells my heart
to put on my shoes and walk on out.

My mother never taught me that
that meant that trouble was brewing
and that I should listen.

She never told me to listen to
the insistent hum of footsteps in my dreams,
trotting on paths I'd never been on.
She never told me that this meant
it was my time to get stepping.

My mother taught me how to love.
To love with my all.

To give my all.
And that is what I do.
I love till I'm all loved out.
Till I've stripped myself bare.
Till all I am,
is a smouldering fireball of love...

And when I do leave.
I leave with just the pair of shoes on my feet.
I leave with my soul in tatters
and my heart still on my sleeve
ready to play catch with the next.

My mother never taught me how to leave.
And when I do leave,
I leave with cast out love and a heart that's unsure of
what to do next.

**—Kearoma Desiree (Mido) Mosata,
Motswana**

"Girls compete with each other, women empower each
other."
— Shira Hirschman Weiss

Authenticity

Complete and open honesty
Open to all life's possibility

Living without need for pretence
No need for self-defence

Self-love accepted
Self-care expected

Be at peace with your life
Avoid unnecessary strife

Living as yourself, free
With your own identity

Free of expectations
Mutually beneficial relations

Live a life of balance
Give happiness a chance

Reject materialism
Fight perfectionism

Hold on to your rights
Keep goals within sight

Speak your mind when needed
Only then can your words be heeded…

Live in your reality
Fostering creativity

Receptive to spirituality
Living a life of generosity

Letting your life be
One of authenticity

— Debbie Johnson, USA

"Women can play a more influential role in society, by being who they are authentically, embracing femininity in its natural state not the way society today pressure women to be - be authentically gentle, beautiful, empathetic, passionate, emotional and strong all at the same time and grounded in faith. We are enough."
—Ruth Ekong, Britain / Nigeria

My Body is a Heritage Site...

A glorious monument shaped by the arc of my hips,
the fullness of my breasts, the curve of my smile and
the coil of my hair.

My body is scarred by stretch marks tattooed on legs
that stretch too wide to accommodate a man who will
never love me with the unwavering devotion I
deserve.

My body is home to a face that carries pain in its
brown eyes whenever the mistakes I make pass me in
the street and all I can smell on them is the foul stench
of regret.

My body is insecurities and inadequacy when my
stomach spills over the band of my jeans in winter
and the beauty in the brownness of my skin is
mercilessly reduced an insulting "you're pretty for a
dark girl" comment.

My body is a constant raging battle of yearning for a
bigger bra size, a smaller waistline and a larger
backside that defies the proportions of my genetically
inherited frame.

My body carries a head with a halo of unruly thick black hair that crackles when a comb gets caught up in its kink and resists the fingers of a man attempting to run his hands through it.

My body is joy and reckless abandon in the laughing lines etched on the sides of my mouth and the crinkle of my eyes when I smile.

My body is freedom and hope in the lightness of my feet when I dance and the richness of my voice when I speak.

My body is rejection in the desperate grip of my fingers around my phone and the elusiveness of sleep combined with twisted anticipation as I wait for that "I love you" message I'll never receive….

My body is the flag of liberation that boasts freedom that was never really won which is evidenced by the struggle for respect by marginalised and hyper-sexualised black women who, contrary to the music videos of pop culture, are worth more than the curves that shape their bodies.

My body is covered by skin etched with words of love and words of hate, and lies and truth, and blessings and curses that were thoughtlessly uttered to me and can never be taken back.

My body is beauty and perfection in the determined strength of my stride, the promise of life in my womb, and the graceful endurance of pain in the precious vulnerability of childbirth.

My body is faith, forgiveness, grace and unconditional love in the words and promises written to me and printed in the pages of the New Testament.

My body is a cage holding hostage a heart that has surrendered its self to the palms of unworthy lovers who defiled the purity of its innocence and caused it to harden.

My body is bitterness and lack of self-worth resulting from starvation of love and social media overconsumption and quenching of the insatiable thirst for material things.

My body is a living symbol that bleeds the blood of a man whose greed and lust betrayed my mother.

My body is a human sponge that soaks up violence and abuse in its flesh….

My body is a unique reflection of the world's critical hatred of difference.

My body is a quiet rebellion led by women who refuse to be silenced.

My body is host to a mind that will always remember, A mind that creates art, a mind that will live on in history.

My body is a heritage site...

A paradoxical celebration of a legacy whose story has just begun.

— Cheryl Zvikomborero Musimwa, Zimbabwe

"Remember always that you not only have the right to be an individual, you have an obligation to be one."
— Eleanor Roosevelt

Dear Diary

Funny almost scary, how your depth always
swallows me.

But how do you escape depth when you love
drowning

Almost explains why I can't seem to escape the sound
of pen kissing trails on paper

Virtually pointing to the place between the tracks of
your skin
Where a hummingbird found her wings

See, dear diary, it's from the seams of your spine
I saw her burst right out of my ribCAGE,
watched her finally embrace her pulchritude

Dear Diary, It was always her
She was always me
It's in the tracks of your skin I met her face to face
And Dear Diary she is beautiful.

**— Xolani Shekhinah Msimango, South
Africa**

One Woman

One woman
can birth a nation
lead an army
negotiate a peace
while standing tall
guiding

One woman
can hold a child
as they cry over
a loss, a cut, a bully
while standing at the stove
cooking dinner for her family
serving

One woman
can stop an epidemic
heal a broken heart
sooth a painful shoulder
while studying medicine
always learning how to do better
growing

One woman
can show the way to country
head up an industry
start a revolution
while sitting
in the halls of power
and at home
leading…..

One woman
can pray for love, food, family
grow a garden
plant a tree
while expressing gratitude
for all that there is
for her loving

And some women with courage
and vision
Do

—Kimberly Burnham, Spokane, WA, USA

"Honor your daughters. They are honorable."
—Malala Yousafzai

Amanda's Dream

In a world of brothers,
where home shifts
and family shifts and home
is "that place" –
shelter for homeless families like hers,
Amanda smiles -- and dreams

the same dream, over and over,
of sisters to talk with,
share with, guide in the passage
from girl to woman.
Amanda of the sweet smile and
murmuring laugh, who rides a bus
to faraway school, dresses
in clothes no one else wants,
lives a life no one covets.
A sister. Not so much to ask.

I can be here today,
be your sister today. But tomorrow
I go back to my life
you to yours –
in your world of brothers
where home shifts

and family too –
remarkable that you
still smile, still dream.

— Linda Simone, San Antonio, TX, USA

"As women I believe our strength lies in our femininity that which makes us women. We need to embrace ourselves more, appreciate our feminine side and love ourselves, that way we can edify ourselves and those around us. We can only truly inspire change through being genuine and that is by acting like women and assuming our roles in society as women."
— Tanyaradzwa (Ty'ra Vanadis) Masaire, Zimbabwe

"The history of all times, and of today especially, teaches that… women will be forgotten if they forget to think about themselves."
—Louise Otto

My African Self

They asked me why my nose was so I wide?
I replied its width allows me to breathe in deeply, to
breathe in deeply everything life throws at me before
I slowly exhale. React.

And why my two front teeth were so wide apart- You
see not only are they wide apart they are strong.
Strong, from the bones that I crush daily.
And their distance, it reminds me everyday of how
my brothers and sisters across the continent are so far
apart- be it in the language they speak or the type of
rice they use to make their jollof? We are still one.
And we still come from the same strong roots.

My knees and elbows? The darkness you mean?
That's cause even though my melanin glistens in the
sun there are parts that are not perfect. And that in
itself, my mother taught me is the real meaning of
perfection.

How come I always stood so tall? Oh that's just me
channeling my inner iroko, reminding everyday me
that I come from a land where trees are tall and
mighty. Reminding me everyday to be just that.

Your lips then? They are so thick! At this point laughed. You see not only does lipstick look amazing on them. I look in the mirror and I see a weapon. The weapon that my heroes used to find their freedom. I see them and I see revolution.

— Amina Hussain El-Yakub, Nigeria

"Feminism isn't about making women stronger. It is about changing the way the world perceives that strength."
—G.D Anderson

"Women can be powerful and influential by being unapologetic about their abilities, simply put just let women be who they want to be. It is wrong to say they can be more influential in owning businesses and flourishing in the work place without giving them the freedom to be influential wherever they choose whether as career women or as homemakers. So, to me a women's influence starts when the world allows her to be true to herself without the need of any sort of validation, because she is already great."
— Xolani (X) Msimango, South Africa

Deceit

With champagne and roses it began
Then promises of travel and jewels
I never knew how happy I could be
But some of us are born to be fools

An expensive house and brand new car
I felt treated like I was a queen
As I travelled here and there
In a chauffeur-driven limousine

A romantic candlelight dinner awaited
He was three hours late getting home
Smelling of alcohol and women's perfume
Obviously, he had found time to roam

Serving dried out dinner and warm wine
I tried my best to hide my suspicion
But his complaints about over-cooked dinner
Brought me to tears and desperation

I tried to chat in a light-hearted tone
But he lacked interest or even a reply
Making continued conversation hard
He must have realized why

The night became more uncomfortable
With each moment that we dined
I uselessly tried to force a smile
But his temper he did find…..

He called me a bitch, a slut, a whore
His glass smashed against the wall
His fist struck my left cheek hard
Causing me to stumble and fall

The next day came a floral bouquet
Along with a note of apology
Apparently, he expected forgiveness
That a few flowers would set him free

The cycle of abuse intensified
Becoming more violent every time
The night he dislocated my shoulder
The time to leave him was prime

The police took my statement in the ER
Domestic charges led to his arrest
He was sentenced to eighteen months
Before his release, I packed, heading west

I found a successful career
But found it hard to trust anyone
I finally gave it a try though
Now I'm happy with my husband and son.

— Debbie Johnson, USA

A girl says her worth, a woman acts her worth.
—Theletter.org

"Jennifer Lawrence, a Hollywood actress once said in an interview, "A powerful woman is someone who exudes confidence and can be tough but fair and kind," she says, "And also knows how to get what she wants."
I believe confidence, toughness, fairness and kindness are deeply rooted in the heart of a woman and the woman who knows how to use these is truly powerful."
—Charlotte Addison, Ghana

"Life is not measured by the number of breaths we take, but by the moments that take our breath away."
—Maya Angelou

Something of Everything

You have something of a fire in your eyes
A song in your thighs
A journey in your feet
A tomorrow in your belly

You have something of a dance in your buttocks
An art in your words
A crown in your hair
A forever in your mind

You have something of the sun on your skin
The living in your hands
The drumbeat of battle in your heart
The memories of what's to come on your brow

You have something
You are that something
That hard to define
That world in a grain of sand
The passage of life.

— Cathrine (Cat) Chidawanyika Makuvise, Zimbabwe

Leave Me Alone

Leave me alone to the high of the peaks,
Along the floating clouds of the sky,
Leave me from the clutches of
Poisonous tentacles of bondage of men,
Leave me free from the cage of humiliation,
Make me fly high with the spirit of freedom,
Leave me to flow calm as a wave of serenity,
And unite with the vast sea of wisdom,
Leave me alone to unfold the petals of love,
And bloom as a wonderful flower of joy......

— Latha Y., India

"The key to playing a more influential role in society in my opinion is unity. Patriarchy unfortunately is the bedrock of many societies, and as such women are generally excluded. To change this, women need to all come together unite in girl power, have one voice, and demand to be heard."
—Amina Hussain El-Yakub, Nigeria

"Women first need to realize that their existence is not complementary to a man's, their very lives are not to be a helper but to make their own impact on the world. Too many times women take the role of servant when their prowess is needed as so much more. One thing that needs to change is always identifying as just mothers, wives, sisters, as if a woman's existence is only valid when in relationship to another's. Women are powerful because they are s much stronger than they like to put on because they have just slipped into the weaker gender role but this is a lie. There is nothing weak about a woman whether physical or emotional, being a relational being is not weak and neither is childbirth. There much more that women can do in society because they are capable and not because they are being tolerated. Men like to say hell cannot match a woman scorned as if our whole lives are a bunch of emotions then deny this fiery nature in everything else."

—Cathrine (Cat) Chidawanyika Makuvise,
Zimbabwe

"A smile is the most beautiful curve on a woman's body."
— Bob Marley

My Country

Your name means House of Stone,
yet I have felt your walls weakening for years.
Your people used to walk with heads held high,
speak, scream and shout boastfully of you,
now they hang their heads and drag their feet,
whispering about how they plan to leave you.
Those that love you worked for you with gleaning
pride,
planning and building empires.
Now the very same people walk your streets on
eggshells,
unsure of their fate.
They still smile though,
they smile as they hold fast to the memories of how
great you were,
they smile as they hold on to the hope of how grand
you will be in the days to come,
They pray for your healing.
They pray for your restoration.
You have always been that magnificent kind of
beautiful,
and you will be again.
You have always had a matchless love that resides in
the heart of your people,

that warmth will radiate again.

This surgery you are going through is a necessary pain,

All the suffering, the hate you have endured is not in vain,

They still love you even though they leave,

They still love you even though they speak ill of you

They just miss the you that kept them safe behind strong walls,

They want to sing songs of your redemption

I want to sing songs of your redemption.

—Rutendo Matewu (Heiressru) Tigere, Zimbabwe

"The most important starting point in being influential is speaking out. Often, women are told to be silent observers of the world and once we find the confidence to use our voices more, the world will be forced to listen and therein will our influence in society grow."

— Cheryl Zvikomborero Musimwa, Zimbabwe

The Elusive One

You slip my warm embrace
Like a shy bride
I tread fast to merge with you
Your pace is faster, your gait swifter
Do you fear that I would enmesh you in my tangle?
You evade, dodge, and remain without reach
I resume my trail, I don't wish you to leave
You are within arms reach, yet far
I stalk and try to seize you in my firm clasp
You sneak past, playing the sport
every time my hand reaches out to touch you,
feel you.
Your form fascinates me, your contour entices me
I am drawn to your charm, your enigma.
Why don't you yield even as I plead?
Just one time, let me touch you, feel you for once
You are spiteful, malicious, hurtful
You remain the unattainable,
I have faithfully courted you in all earnestness
All these years, you chose to stay aloof
As a child, I was bemused
As I grew up, I was enthralled
Never once did you budge to give in to my wishes
In the light of the day nor in the dark of the night

Though you linger, my constant companion, my
semblance
A delightful silhouette you are
Who mirrors my image without fail
As I am tormented by my thoughts
You are devoid of such worries
How I wish I could coalesce with you
Should I then have no qualms
About the tiring world!

— Sandhya Padmanabhan, India

*"Women are clear-headed, they are more creative and for
this reason, sometimes, also more fragile."*
— Emma Bonino

*"Think like a queen. A queen is not afraid to fail. Failure is
another steppingstone to greatness."*
—Oprah Winfrey

Formation

With joy I embraced my swollen bosom,
My expanded skin and king Kong feet
A daily dream of whose features would be stamped
on you,
Ingesting the very meals you make me crave
One which makes me a hungry lion;
Bitter or sweet responding to them as you would,
Taking them in or bringing them out.
A ceased blood flow that last as long,
My routine and joyous inflicting lifestyle,
One I embrace as you form in me.

— Ruth (Anastasia Ruth) Yacim, Nigeria

"Women should be allowed to get an education; it is unfortunate that even today, thousands of women are not allowed to go to school yet and are, instead, married off or made to do housework while their male counterparts are given the chance to learn and build the foundation for their future."
— Sasha (Bad Bunny) Leigh Coutinho, Zimbabwe

Strong Enough

In my weakness, you see me as strong
On our bad days, you think I have super powers
On my worse days, you assume am strong enough
You think I can pull through whatever
No matter what it is
However, I keep pulling strength from a source
One which never ends or causes me weakness
One through which I do all things
All things you think I have super powers for as a
mum
One I want you to embrace too
As one day, I would need you to take from that
source and be my strength.

— Ruth (Anastasia Ruth) Yacim, Nigeria

"Women need to appreciate their own selves and express
boldly in matters of home and state. If women exercise this
freedom, they can create wonders, work miracles."
— Sandhya Padmanabhan, India

Feminine Heroics

Fragile, incapable of taking charge, afraid to get her
hands dirty,
Destined to stand in a man's shadow, just a few
Entirely untrue and misconstrued stereotypes of a
woman,
for she is none of that. How could she who
Manages to carry the burden of a child growing
within her
be weak, yet she is
Able to get back on her feet six weeks after twelve
hours plus
of unimaginably painful
Labour? How can she who raises a child from a
murmuring
bundle of joy to an
Enigmatic leader, preacher, charismatic teacher, be
incompetent when she planted the seed
of imagination and nurtured the resulting seedling
to a towering

Green mound of potential, a canopy of obscure ideas,
movements, progress,
statuesque, thriving branches of

Innovation, a sturdy trunk of support, reliability?
What could be the
Reason for wanting to keep such a positive influencer,
possible game changer,
gifted mind shaper,
Lower, and not equal to, her male counterparts? After
all these centuries?

Would it not make way for better days that we, for
decades,
have wished for if
Our sisters, mothers, daughters, could walk free along
these streets
without fear of
Molestation, violation of all kinds, all demonstrations
of disregard for the
traumatisation caused by the
Abuse they suffer at their fathers', brothers' uncles'
hands, the man
who was supposed to protect her
from the evils of this land,
Now taking advantage of her inability to stand up for
herself
and speak against the…

Monstrosities that every week she endures or tires to
run from,

or avoids

Or tries to forget once they are done to her, telling herself it's her fault. Who is she to

Trust when her knight in shining armour is her every night's most paralysing fear?

How does she cope with it all? The rapid changes, the responsibilities;

are they not too much?

Every day from the time she can understand words she is told to tone her true self down,

lest she threaten the man.

Running around in the mud is not a luxury for her,

for "Girls should not get dirty."

Skirts hinder her movements as she tries to do as a child should

do in their childhood,

Indulging in rough games, jumping around, carefree, climbing up trees, without fear

of what any passer-by below her might see. Alas…

She grows past the height of her father's hip, past her mother's waist,

And a new discovery of her body is made.

Tiny red-brown spots startle her one morning, one afternoon, one evening,

as she stares at her underwear,
Evidence of womanhood finally coming to her,
a mark of her next adventure,
Readying her for her first love, first kiss, first heart
break, first time...

First, hopefully only, marriage, first child. How does
she cope with all the pain,
along with high school drama,
Reading through what she is taught in class, racing in
a one hundred metre dash,
Interpreting words in a language she does not speak?
How
does she manage to balance
Endless academic and extracurricular activities and
still muster up the energy
to cook and
Nourish her family, feeding mouths that often
overlook
her effort and forget to show their
gratitude,
Dumping their gravy stained plates in the sink for her
to clean,
pretending they have not seen
her tired eyes, yearning to be
allowed to close and dream.

Graciously, she goes about this day by day; she needs
the survival skill
in future anyway.
Rarely does she complain about her position, but
when she does,
she brings up a solution,
Actively altering the order of things and teaching
each of the living being
around her

Necessary lessons on how to keep their possessions
neat and tidy, how to chop vegetables,
Dust the furniture, sweep the dust off the floor,
she does all this and more
for she knows that…

Moaning and whining will only create discordant
noise
rather than teach boys
to be domesticated.
Oh, how does she handle society's mercilessly high
pressure
to morph her body forcefully into something "better",
Take the cruel laughter directed at her imperfection,
the directed at her
again when

Her face is covered and transformed slightly,
temporarily
by make-up?
Every day she wakes up and cries bitterly at the sight
of her
hard-to-do hair
Ready to shave her scalp as bare as her legs are
expected to be
all the way up above the hem of her underwear.

Why does she tolerate it all? Or does she really?
for later she rebels and shapes her own
Independent, unique form, no longer blending in
with the norm,
Facing the world in her now adult body
refusing to fall for any folly
Entranced in her ambitions to pursue her Master's
Degree
graduate, climb up the corporate ladder
and become the Queen Bee……

How amazing that she does all this and more,
but, maybe, not so shocking for
Evidently, only a woman can push it all aside
and still stand tall with pride
Red bottom stiletto heels, six inches high and that,
ladies and gents, is why

On this day we celebrate her, The Woman, the victor, the heroes of our lives.

— Sasha (Bad Bunny) Leigh Coutinho, Zimbabwe

"In ancient times, it was always the place of the Queen Mother to advise and direct the King of a nation. I think that this fact emphasizes that women today have an incredible capacity for leadership. I look around at my friends, my sisters, my mother, my coworkers, and I see not feral Amazons, but women who truly tap into who they are as human beings, using their incredible ability to sympathize and understand others from all over the world in order to effect change. In today's world, I see that women will lead us into a future of understanding and compromise, not a time of trying to prove other people wrong or squash other peoples' abilities."
—Michelle L. Schmid, USA

"Life shrinks or expands in proportion to one's courage."
—Anais Nin

Women of the World

8th of March is International Woman's Day.
Internet portals are pretty and nice,
full of flowers, compliments and red hearts.
It's for free, just copy - paste

A married woman was stoned in the mountain
village.
She fell in love with another man.
She forgot that she had an owner.
Her husband threw the first stone.
The world is silent.

A young girl was hanged in the big city.
She deserved to die, her eyes were beautiful.
A crowd of men surrounded and raped her.
She asked for it.
The world is silent.

A child did not survive her wedding night.
The girl died, it happens.
All was in accordance with the law.
The old man paid well for a virgin.
The world is silent.

The schoolgirls were kidnapped and sold.
The slaves have their price.
The sexual toys have become cheaper lately,
the law of demand and supply works.
The world is silent.

In the villages of bachelors there are no women.
Dowry is expensive, abortion is cheap.
All female embryos were removed.
Each family wants a son.
The world is silent.

He gave her a rose in the morning
and a bruise under the eye in the evening.
It was her fault, she deserved to be punished
- the soup was too salty.

— **Alicja Maria Kuberska, Poland**

*There is considerable evidence that women's education and
literacy tend to reduce the mortality rates of children.*
—Anartya Sen, Development as Freedom, 2000, pg
195)

During the First Shave of the Season

The initial stroke
leaves her leg new, smooth
like a baby's fat cheek, unkissed
by the wind, her wintercoat's absence
puts her nerves on end.

The second drag
of the purple razor
just so along the line of bone
trails a river of blood to the drain

bright and becoming pink
she has successfully skinned
herself, friendless flesh exposed
raw, her struggles lie open.
she tries to staunch the flow.

she barely feels
like a relationship gone bad, pain
remains the instant after
water courses through the wound,

cleansed, the cut becomes memory-scar
left as a reminder white pure

rising above surrounding skin-tone
recalling everything done
now overcome.

—Michelle L. Schmid, Rochester, MN, USA

"Women already play an influential role just that their light is over-shadowed. One way to get society to realize this is by teaching children from an early age to respect women and not taint women and downplay their amazing traits. According to me, women are already powerful. We see this in our mother's eyes, in the words of guidance they give us and in all the other amazing women we come across. Women's power comes from something only God can explain."
—Kearoma Desiree (Mido) Mosata, Motswana

"Whatever you do, be different – that was the advice my mother gave me, and I can't think of better advice for an entrepreneur. If you're different, you will stand out."
– Anita Roddick

Days

Days like a necklace of grey pearls
that stretch leaving marks and signs on the body.
Days of two faces
where one is the world and nobody at the same time.

Nothing there
no judgement
no prayer
accompanies the void
the multitude that guards this reflection.

Days walled by mystery
and death ripens in every corner
in each contraction and redoubling
as in a fish recently slumbering.

Days in which there is no one offering up a surprise
the desertion
the coldness of the watch
days in which chaos resounds and explodes in the
mirror

— Itzela Sosa, Mexico
Translated by Glenna Luschei

Strangers or Loneliness

In the seductive colours of nightfall,
a shield of silence is defeated only by tiny crickets,
as every hour gives me another wrinkle.
Watching other peoples' fairy tales on fast-forward in
my mind's eye.
I see loneliness approach
and I start to miss strangers.
People who I have met during the active sessions of
my imagination.
Tall dark men in tailor made suits.
I miss stone faces, that are sometimes cracked by
smiling lips.
Slits that replace eyes, making you wonder if they are
optically competent,
myopic they turn out.
Light flexible tongues that refuse to give in to the
weight of lies that roll off them, dribbling
honey.
Hands that possess pleasure in their expanse.
Lips that taste like sweet poison.
Making death an attractive saviour when the poison
becomes toxic to your heart and it starts punishing
you with physical pain.

Nights on the bathroom floor hoping the mirror will say something different other than ugly & not good enough.

I miss strangers that I already know from my past. People whose presence I loath and desire simultaneously.

— Vimbai Josephine Lole, Zimbabwe

"Women can play a more influential role in society ... The How part ... by being educated, being elevated or empowered economically and socially (ie) Marxist and social feminism. Being competitive and wise in jobs (ie) engineering and the hard works that man usually do. The What part ... regarding themselves as important and not undermining themselves, and realising their superiority in the family and or community."
—Toiwa (P. A. Tunechi) Petronella, Zimbabwe

"I know God will not give me anything I can't handle. I just wish that He didn't trust me so much."
– Mother Teresa

The Potter

Dirty and unkempt
She carries her basin
Waiting for people to call out to her
Her feet bare
She walks hurriedly through the market.
Looking pale and frail, thin and slim
Yet, an iota of strength has she
To carry her customers wares.
A pale-looking boy like she
Her baby to be precise
Sleeps at three back
Wrapped with filthy clothes
With no education
Waking up periodically to say
"Maa, Maa, am hungry".
She pays no attention
Pats him on the butt
A sign to say "shut up".

She moves steadily ahead
No time for babies.
She suddenly comes across someone with her wares
Quickly loads her basin and walks a long distance
Receiving only a dime as wage……

She smiles happily
Alas! There's something to feed on
She mumbles a thank
And speeds off to wait for another.
Night falls
Her dilemma begins
Nowhere to lay her head
On cardboards she lays with her baby
On a deserted space of a shop till daybreak.
She hardly sleep, I can say
Has to cope with the dangerous bites of mosquitoes
All night she spends
Driving away those hungry and blood-thirsty devils.
Morning comes
Ready to face another bustling day in order to survive
with child.
She's the lady we know
With neither education nor ego
She is the porter
The Kayaye.

— Patience (Nana Ama) Osei Bonsu, Accra, Ghana

From A Mother's Lips

The first time I saw your face;
My heart stopped then started to race;
Though your birth was the result of my disgrace;
In my heart you now held a permanent place.

Your teeth grew and you learnt to smile;
You grew up so fast but it took me a while;
To see a young woman with a crazy style;
With her room a mess and dirty clothes in a pile.

Your grades began to drop;
The boys whistling would never stop;
I was your shelter I was your rock;
But your intense hatred gave me a shock;

Oh yes he keeps talking;
My dear is he listening?
When you lay on that table bleeding;
Was it not I who held your hand when you came back
running?

My mirrors image the apple of my eye;
One day you will know there is always a battle inside;
There will be tears you will have to hide;

When a tiny hand is clutching your side.
This is a letter to my daughter;
I will read it when she is older;
With every second my love grows stronger;
These are the words from your mother.

— Chiwawa Fungai (Leeyone) Manana, Zimbabwe

"Women should stop trying to prove themselves as good enough to be second rate males. We were created equal but not the same, we have different roles and women should take pride in that, be the best they can and offer society the beautiful personalities and contributions that men cannot. We have become so busy as women trying to prove that we can do everything men can, in the process losing our uniqueness. We are not meant to do all a man can, but to do all a man cannot. What makes a woman powerful is the uniqueness she offers, her relevance. She is a natural nurturer who as an emotional creature thrives on emotional expression that in turn relieves stress and frustrations."
—Vimbai Josephine Lole, Zimbabwe

A Philosopher and a Poet

they met between heaven and earth
at the place where time and matter are irrelevant
at a higher level of abstraction
they overcame the barriers of the real world

he brought a white canvas and philosophical maxims
she brought the paint brushes
and a handful of dreams in words
they painted the picture in many shades of blue
they poured their thoughts and feelings into the ether

he sketched the outlines of life with a bold navy blue
line
she filled the background with gentle azure brushes.
together they added a few colorful spots of
astonishment.
his eyes are hazel and hers are green

**— Alicja Maria Kuberska, Inowrocław,
Poland**

Hearts

I had so desired to place her into his big, strong
hands…
to be the keeper till eternity because he wanted to be
the One.
But he never learned how to treasure her.
Hearts.

Words that would melt glaciers and a touch smoother
than Cadburys made me
long to pour into him like a Baileys liquor, the love
that was already seeping from
my veins…
Quench. His. Thirst..

Colgate smile…oh smile…bright canines and molars
that matched a glisten in his
eye had my heart on edge, pounding and ready.
So I unlocked my gates and let him play with her…
Play, pluck and pilfer he did, till he was bored and
my crimson, beating organ no
longer amused him.

Blind to how she worked and the little things that
made her beat a little stronger.

Tick faster and faster and faster... Pumping the
vibrant colours back into her
cheeks. Oh how she would blush...

But like a rebel kid handed a beautiful rose, he left my
petals scattered on the
ground. Pieces of me in places I never knew existed.
My heart, now colourless and bruised, broken and
used. Dirty.
No longer an eye-catching red, rather a shade of grey.

Almost missed her, unrecognisable among the rubble
and decaying waste...
Couldn't pick her up..
Couldn't bear to put her back in my chest.
I had failed to protect the greatest treasure I had to
offer....
I dust her off..., barely warm and beating. A slow,
dull ember.
Solitary on the ground.
Take the pulsating organ in my arms.
Emotions and hurt still spilling from her aorta.

"Do you want to keep her?"
As if referencing a stray, a voice says...
"But what if I lose her again?" I exclaim

You could never lose a heart that's forever found in
Me….
Veins encapsulated with my Word and divine amour
flowing in beautiful
harmony with your plasmas.
You see, I should be the only love that sets you free.
The only Master with the key to unlock the gates of
your psyche.

Trust. In. Me. Only
For I formed her intricacies, shaped her arteries.
It's my blood that stains the inner walls of your heart.
Crimson red denoting the price of my sacrifice.
Only my touch could bring you back to life...

Place your heart in my hands.
Let me be the One.
Love Christ.

— Ruth Ekong, Britain / Nigeria

*"A woman's power lies within. The moment we realise that
we are exceptional and unique creatures who are not in
competition with anyone, our power and strength will spill
from the inside out and we will realise our full potential."*
— Cheryl Zvikomborero Musimwa, Zimbabwe

Fire

"You just had to go on and ruin a good thing
Didn't you?!"
She said like a fire breathing dragon,
standing guard at the foot of her majesty's castle.

She hones this...
Pryrokinectic ability like a fire bending avatar.
Spewing infernos,
with the precision of a heat seeking missile.

They say she's a women scorned.
Really just another casualty of war.

But the beauty of loving her guarded heart
lies in the pulchritudinous nature of her gracious
soul.
Simply because,
behind the incinerating walls of fiery furry
she kept a treasure that was infinite.

Her true self.

— Xolani (X) Msimango, South Africa

Woman Appreciation

When it's winter outside
I need not look for shelter
'coz in you I have a place to hide
So long as we are together

You are the warm sunshine
After stormy weather
That brings soothing calm
And makes everything better

Demure though you are
In you is a fierce fighter
Whose spirit blazes fire
Making you the best protector

You are and always will be woman
The essence of this world
Around whom all life rotates

**— Tanyaradzwa (Ty'ra Vanadis) Masaire,
Zimbabwe**

Cleansing, For Fanny Mbewe

"...they hunted her down...insisted that if she refused to exorcise her dead husband's spirit, she would be blamed every time a villager died."
—Sharon LaFraniere, New York Times, Section A1, May 10, 2005

This is for you, Fanny, and all our sisters
whose spirits are erased
by tradition,
by patriarchies where women are pawns.

From his unmarked grave, even your spouse James
approves
as they drag you from your sister's Malawi hut
for the final funereal ritual – forced sex
with his cousin. They say only this will save
the people of your village from madness, disease,
save you.

How did it feel, still nursing widowhood's wounds,
to submit to savage bondage?

How would you have felt if you refused?
and your countrymen dropped like flies?

Afterward, you washed your most private places,
desperate to ward off AIDs,
hoping to save your children from becoming orphans.

From the front-page photo you
--26 years old, native garb,
arms crossed, feet firmly planted — stare at me.

You are news
not because your slavery is accepted as custom
but because a virus ravages your continent

What are you asking me to do?

— Linda Simone, San Antonio, TX, USA

*"Women can play influential roles in society by actually
stepping up to the challenge society throws at them and
taking every opportunity that comes their way and creating
the very opportunities they need by being creative,
innovative and determined to challenge the status quo and
build a better world for generations."*
—Charlotte Addison, Ghana

Three Years Old Watching the Open Sky

To my mother Magdalena and my grandmother
Lorenza

In mangoes there's always springtime
Is always the sweet liquid light from those months
when one swings
always for a first time
and in your arms
the extension of istle changes
into a pair of wings that gallop and gallop

Yellow is the smell of that house
from never-ending guava three on the path
where the canticle of roosters
on their red march flowered in appointed time
rose through the balconies
until it reached the heart
the breath and the curtains

In that house the corn
grew like a skin that covered our emptiness
the cold from hunger that encircled us
in deep tracks in the streets

there were the corn kernels who gave us a name
kneading our thirst
and the words laid out on the table

In that house
were women's hands
those that with their alchemy
made the wind and vapours dance
those that wove bread ...
oaths
marks in the eyes
all the miracles

In that deep house of yellow aromas
the light entered slowly by the edges
for saying goodbye
for illuminating shadows in the mirrors
the furies of the gods
the white sap of their daughters
and the sacred heart of dying day

That house
rattle of first-born sounds
Mixteco womb that nourished
the walk of those pilgrims
the night always open in their footsteps
the moist sierra that trembled in their pupils

like the night that watched them depart
taking leave of the village
leaving their infancy and their tenderness on the path

It's on the mountain ridges
where the owl tells the fortune of men
who return from the silence of the heights
as dust
It's in the chant where life carries on
opens the door to say

Now is always!
doves are still in the body
pilgrims who seek
who wander....
the incantation is always musical
is a requiem of germinating roots

It's the chant who carry us
to the clay
to the seed
to the always safely warm dream of Tonantzin

In that house musical note
        IS
this smell
everlasting and yellow

a whirlwind that grows
watches us
and irretrievably shakes us
and inhabits us
     IS
that aroma profound
unending
childlike
and yellow

— Itzela Sosa, Mexico

In: Memorias de Intemperie (2010), Instituto de Cultura de Morelos, Colección La Hogaza.

"The crucial step in the life of a woman is the ability to realize her self-worth and that her power is unfathomable. Most women float through their lives with only one purpose and that is to celebrate the achievements of others. The most influential role a woman can play in the society is to build that self-awareness and strength in the heart of a younger woman. If we help our generation today we create a better chance for the generations to come."
—Chiwawa Fungai (Leeyone) Manana, Zimbabwe

276

I put my pen to paper and I knew I was gonna write
you an apology
Thing is I'm not exactly sure what I'm most sorry for
Actually I lied; I do know what I'm most sorry for
I'm sorry you had to be born, born and then subjected
to a life of poverty
A life of struggle simply because your country's men
had over time lost all sense of humanity
They'd simply let all the labor of our heroes past all
go in vain
So you got poorer as they got richer, you got thinner
as they got fatter.
And in the midst of all this, you still dreamed- you lot
were gonna be doctors, lawyers and teachers,
probably our saviors
But on the 14th of April 2014, we crushed those
dreams. And I'm sorry.
I'm sorry we handed you over to faceless cowards
hiding behind a religion of peace, hiding behind the
political greed of your country's men (but that's a
topic for another day).
I'm sorry that you've been reduced to just numbers,
276 girls in captivity for x number of days.
I'm sorry.

I'm sorry that what you had made of life was shattered, that your mother's hearts were shattered. I'm sorry.
You may never forgive us, and whether you do doesn't really matter because history will never forgive us. And for that I am glad.
I'm sorry. And I hope one day your hearts find peace.

— Amina Hussain El-Yakub, Nigeria

"Women who are fortunate enough to live free according to their own minds and hearts not only have an opportunity, but also a responsibility to speak out on behalf of others. Their sisters worldwide who may be silenced by sexism, suppressed by economic circumstances, or enslaved by barbaric cultural practices desperately depend on others to speak out for them. Poetry is one way to raise awareness."
— Linda Simone, San Antonio, TX, USA

"A woman is like a tea bag - you can't tell how strong she is until you put her in hot water."
— Eleanor Roosevelt

Woman

Your shoulders were never meant to slouch so
Your head should keep a crown in place
Why do you bow it so?
It seems to me you are a weapon of mass destruction
wrapped in silk
They just forget to look beyond the silk
All soft ripples following your curves
Like the surface of the ocean hides much
A beautiful cover for the volcano at your core
Your passions repressed always waiting to erupt
You have believed their lies
Listen to fear driven words
They need your shoulders to slump so
To burden you down with the world while they
dominate
The row without you making you the subject
But your head should wear a crown
Never an apologetic tiara
Watered down with fake reasons
A crown all your own
Why have you listened to their lies
Can you not feel YOU trying to push out of you
They give you title after title of servitude
Helping their dreams come true

While you are stuck in the mundane
But look at you
Co-creator with the creator
Bringing forth and nourishing life
You carry the world on the inside
Bringing it forth little by little.......
Generations proceeding from you
And yet, you are even more than that
Capable
Strong
Gifted
Raise your head, woman
Straighten your crown.

— Cathrine (Cat) Chidawanyika Makuvise, Zimbabwe

"A woman's most powerful attribute is her belief that she is made in GOD's image making her extremely beautiful and needing no one else to validate her worth ... "A masterpiece is still a masterpiece even though the lights are off and the room is empty."... A woman who believes and treats herself like a masterpiece is a powerful woman.
—Rutendo Matewu (Heiressru) Tigere, Zimbabwe

From A Warrior's Lips

I can hear the drums;
I can smell the smoke;
That's the beating of my heart;
And the gathering clouds of fallacy.
The crowds are cheering now;
They are thirsty for my blood;
They know my opponent is immeasurable;
I know that my opponent is my doubt.
I hear footsteps;
But I see only one shadow;
The darkness is deceitful;
I thought I was never alone.
Victory screams from the other side;
Fear warns me to hide;
Hate tells me I will never find;
Peace from the other side.
If you start with the river;
You might conquer the ocean;
Such ridicule I have faced;
When I began to drown in the oceans depths.
A hand pulled me out of the water;
Then I heard many voices shouting to each other;
I trotted shyly on their loyal backs;
And crossed the deep waters.

Finally I held victory in my arms;
The scars inflicted by my opponent had finally healed;
Hate was wrong and peace was mine;
I had made it to the other side!

— Chiwawa Fungai (Leeyone) Manana, Zimbabwe

"Women already play an influential role just that their light is over-shadowed. One way to get society to realize this is by teaching children from an early age to respect women and not taint women and downplay their amazing traits. According to me, women are already powerful. We see this in our mother's eyes, in the words of guidance they give us and in all the other amazing women we come across. Women's power comes from something only God can explain."
—Kearoma Desiree (Mido) Mosata, Botswana

"Knowing what must be done does away with fear."
— Rosa Parks

Hope Implied

International implies
women on the opposite side
of the world
a political spectrum
the street
share a world with me

Women implies
that gender is a bonding agent
more important
less than other characteristics
we are connected

Day implies
that for one day
change can happen
chains can be broken
walls can be torn down
we are here in this moment
together…

Poetry implies
words matter, colors, images
dance out of our mouths

we create
each new day
a bond
understanding
and justice
in this international world
of women and men
today and tomorrow.

—Kimberly Burnham, Spokane, WA, USA

"There are many ways to make women powerful. But among all those ways I think that regain the ability to name the world and their own experiences through literature is one of the most powerful and subversive forms to fight against sexism, androcentrism and to destabilize gender structures. Keep on writing and re-making (re-constructing) symbolic and material worlds."
—Itzela Sosa, Mexico

To educate girls is to reduce poverty.
—Former UN Secretary General, Kofi Annan

Fashion

She's the lady of ego, the girl of her prime
She's the centre of attraction, an ogling picturesque.
She's the power which encapsulates the minds and
eyes of men
The magnet which does people in without a choice.
She's the force forcefully penetrating into the hearts
and souls of many
The offer never rejected.
She's what everyone craves for
The highest commodity on the international market.
She's the lady who twists and turns the minds of the
young
Making them vacillate
She's a vagrant, a vagabond
Bringing all vagary.
She's like the slim copper-coloured model in her
pencil heels
Who winds and swings her fine waist to the public
And leaves them with no choice than to comply.
She's the lady of attention, causing more detentions
she's the core of seduction, slowly moving as lava
from a molten volcano magma.
She shines brighter than a constellation, than a zillion
galaxies in the atmosphere

She's complacent, giving no damn about others.
She's the lady with class
Making vulnerable ones kowtow with her whims and
whimpering…..
She's fashion
The lady of generations
She's the inexplicable one
The lady of her time.

— Patience (Nana Ama) Osei Bonsu, Accra, Ghana

"The fastest way to change society is to mobilise the women of the world." — Charles Malik

"Everything about a woman makes her powerful; whether she knows it or not. Women may be known as home makers but they can and should become great advisors to agencies, government and non-government organisation, political parties and so on. Women must not only give advice at home- they can and should do more."
— Ruth (Anastasia Ruth) Yacim, Nigeria

In A Different World

If I could turn back the hands of time there are two
things that I would change: I would unmeet you or
meet you sooner.

My life has changed irreversibly,
I want so much to blame someone or something,
but there's only you and there's only me.
I can't blame you for being sweet, charming or
handsome.
I can however blame myself for allowing myself to
see you as more than just another guy.

But I can blame you for your honesty for sharing your
thoughts and feelings.
I can't blame myself for sharing mine,
I thought that would be it and all would be buried
that night.

That first night which came from that first hello,
led to that first goodbye and then another hello…
That song 'Let's Just Kiss and Say Goodbye'… It's just
a song.
I wanted to say goodbye, we needed to yet after that
moment my world changed-again.

At first it spun round and round then turned up-side-down.
I was determined to forget you,
to not entertain thoughts or do I mean hopes of being in a different world.

Determination wasn't enough, thoughts of you came slowly at first,
then like rushing wind shaking everything in its way and making its presence felt.

I promised myself, I promised you...
I'll stay away from you I said...I wonder if I ever meant it.
Now I find myself here, in this place.

A place I need so much to get away from,
a place I want so much to spend more time in.
A place that would be perfect bliss if it were in a completely different world.

There's so much here that I hate.
I hate that I miss you so much,
it makes me feel weak.
I hate that you make me smile,
it makes me feel so out of control.
I hate that I enjoy talking to you,

I hate that I look forward to your texts,
I hate that you're the best part of my day.

Above all I hate that I love you, because don't know
what to do about it.

—Rutendo Matewu (Heiressru) Tigere, Zimbabwe

"*Powerful women are open, honest and authentic. They know themselves and act accordingly. They don't pretend to be something that they are not and are not people pleasers. To be influential, a good education is essential, and that we use whatever platform we have, for me its poetry, to advocate for rights and causes we feel are important.*"
— Debbie Johnson, USA

"*Confidence, a feeling of self assurance arising from the appreciation of one's own abilities or qualities, is what makes a woman powerful.*"
—Amina Hussain El-Yakub, Nigeria

Pedagogical Dilemma

Passion becomes profession
Moulding young minds
essaying myriad roles
Mentor, guide, facilitator

With feigned dignity and decorum
Step into a space
To be greeted by forty odd faces
A stage to perform

Camouflage your stark identity
Mask your emotions
Transform into a character
Please a skeptical audience
That fall prey to Idiosyncrasies, is it truly me?

I question myself, Do I confuse or convince?
Enthralled at the reception
I perform better by the day

Unique is the style
Teaching, an art, aesthetically display
An array of skills
Wax eloquent on matters familiar and unfamiliar

Sheer gift of the gab!
I succeed as I am received.

— Sandhya Padmanabhan, Bangalore, India

"As women we need to believe that what we have achieved, the experiences we have had are worth sharing. There is nothing more encouraging than hearing the story of someone who has been exactly where you are and come out of it stronger and better. There is nothing more motivating than hearing the story of someone who was exactly where you are, struggling with what you are struggling with but turned their life around and rose above it. Women can impact society by sharing of themselves and empowering each other."
—Rutendo Matewu (Heiressru) Tigere, Zimbabwe

"I am too intelligent, too demanding, and too resourceful for anyone to be able to take charge of me entirely. No one knows me or loves me completely. I have only myself"
— Simone de Beauvoir

Royalty

There is a crown lying idle in the gutter
Mud spluttered jewels
Value lost, precious metals, lost lustre

There are crowns lying idle in the gutter
Reduced to valueless, mud spluttered jewels
Corroded special metals that have lost their lustre
Whose beauty now lies beyond face values (eyes,
priceless, rhyme with jewels)

We live in the city of queens
But no one in the palace resides
Only fleeting ghosts of what once was
And echoes of former eras memories

The dark ages reign obliterating the suns' rays
Leaving empty streets like arid savannahs
Hope is plenty scarce like the hunger in people's eyes
And the smell of decay emanating from hope
deadened souls

Dreams only occur in the visions of the ambitious
Those highest in the lands food chains
Who prey on the aspirations of the weak and hopeless

And devour the fruit of their strenuous labours

But try to break you though they might
Never keep the throne out of sight
'Coz it's yours not by favour but by right
Queen- pick up your crown and hold on tight

The world is at its' darkest- be its light
Let your strength shine forth and bear its weight
Be that flavour – the earths' salt
Soothing broken hearts and killing spite

This is not going to be an easy ride
But let not your feet falter or abandon the fight
'Coz victory is yours not by favour but by right
Queen-You are royalty- pick up your crown and hold
on tight!

— Tanyaradzwa (Ty'ra Vanadis) Masaire, Zimbabwe

"A feminist is anyone who recognizes the equality and full humanity of women and men."
— Gloria Steinem

Push for the Rights of Women

You uncouth people,
You've set your mind to oppress women,
You're the cause of our tears because of your pride,
We continue weeping for our rights,
Push for the rights of women!
You tickle each others fancy looking for ways to
oppress us more,
We're now employers in your absence,
For years we've been labouring, hoping you'd see our
importance,
Look within and remember where you're from,
And prioritise what is of utter importance,
Push for the rights of the woman!
We're so confused!
We don't know what to do,
And we stand flabbergasted!
You are the authors of confusion that hold women
outcasts,
Where is the heart of togetherness?
We want equality with you,
To rub shoulders with you.
Give women opportunities! Give them the worth they
deserve!
Push for the rights of women!

Make haste people
Make haste government
Make haste saviours
Find ways of putting yourselves on the map by
pushing the rights of women
Give! Build!
Give them joy by granting them their rights,
And by giving them their place,
Because that is where they'll flourish .
Push for the rights of women!

— Toiwa (P. A. Tunechi) Petronella, Pumula South, Bulawayo, Zimbabwe

Translated by Xeshelihle R. Ncube and Silindile Ndlovu

"Education and consciousness of our connection to other men and women, animals, and the natural world make women powerful."
— Kimberly Burnham, USA

To My Love

I didn't realize marriage to you
would be a roller- coaster ride,
those shrieks, thrills, fears, laughter
would be fearsome and also lovable.
There were dreams & nightmares too, but
After all these years of being dated & mated,
sharing, caring, loving, hating...
My feelings have never dwindled...
I keep falling in love all over again...

— Usha Krishnamurthy, India

"Women can play a more influential role in society, by being who they are authentically, embracing femininity in its natural state not the way society today pressure women to be - be authentically gentle, beautiful, empathetic, passionate, emotional and strong all at the same time and grounded in faith. We are enough."
—Ruth Ekong, Britain / Nigeria

Colour Blind

I want to smell blue
The colour that my fiancé's
girlfriend looks good in, making
her lady lumps even more defined.

I want to smell blue
The colour of the ink that wrote in
perfect writing to tell me it was not me. It was him.

I want to smell blue
The colour of the door he shut in
my face after he dragged me out of
our house; me screaming, begging
him to stop this abuse, him all
calm and soothing, telling me he
never meant to hurt me.

I want to smell blue.
The colour of his favourite shirt I
used to wear as a dress during the
long nights he travelled to see his
grandmother who was always down
with the flu.

God! I want to smell blue
because my eyes now refuse to
acknowledge the colour that
embodies the death of my heart
and spirit.

— Vimbai Josephine Lole, Harare, Zimbabwe

"Being a woman is power in and of itself: birth givers, nurtures, mediators, world shakers. The most influential role women can play is accepting their femininity: accepting their difference and embracing their strength, instead of comparing themselves to men, and also building each other up."
—Nyakallo (Azanian_Nile_Lily) Posholi, South Africa

"It's not my responsibility to be beautiful. I'm not alive for that purpose. My existence is not about how desirable you find me."
— Warsan Shire

The Poets

Charlotte Addison, Ghana

Rytersdiary.blogspot.com

Charlotte Addison is a Poet and Writer. She is a member of Writers Project Ghana and Walk The Talk Poetry Organization. Her works have been published in 'Echoes from OLA', 'The Siren Magazine'; both are magazines where she served as Deputy Editor and Head of Editing, respectively. She has performed at 'Read Me a Poem in the Candle Light', 'Showdown with the Dons of Poetry with Dorian Paul D', 'A Poetry Note to Injustice' and has also performed on 'Writers Project' on Citi FM-Ghana and 'Open Air Theatre 'on Radio Univers.

Kimberly (Nerve Whisperer) Burnham, Spokane, WA, USA

NerveWhisperer.Solutions/Poetry

Life spirals. As a 28-year-old photographer, Kimberly Burnham appreciated beauty. Then an ophthalmologist diagnosed her with a genetic eye condition saying, "Consider what your life will be like if you become blind." Devastating words trickling down into her soul, she discovered a healing path with insight, magnificence, and vision. Today, a poet and neurosciences expert with a PhD in Integrative Medicine, Kimberly's life mission is to change the face of global brain health. Using health coaching, poetry, Reiki, Matrix Energetics, craniosacral therapy, acupressure, and energy medicine, she supports people in their healing from brain, nervous system, chronic pain, and eyesight issues.

Kimberly has been celebrating International Women's Day since the 1980's. With contributions to over 60 books on Amazon, she is a member of the Inner Child Press poetry posse and publishes monthly in *The Year of The Poet*. Her poetry is included in *Healing Through Words; Inspired by Gandhi; Paper Nautilus 2012; Music Carrier of Intention in 49 Jewish Prayers;* and many more collections.

Sasha (Bad Bunny) Leigh Coutinho, Zimbabwe

Twitter.com/bad_bunny97

When asked about women of influence and power, Sasha Leigh Coutinho said, "Society should encourage women to take on leadership roles if they possess the required character traits rather than continuing women to pursue careers that conform to stereotypical role of woman (cooking, cleaning, etc.) These jobs are also beneficial but not every woman is destined for such a career path and those that suit "men's" jobs should be taught how to and allowed to pursue such career paths."

Ruth Ekong, Britain / Nigeria

Whatruthysaidnext.wix.com/sabelleame
Twitter.com/justruthy

A London, UK resident, Ruth Ekong, is the founder of Christian creative arts organisation, Rhema Arts UK and performs at various open mic events in London.

Amina Hussain El-Yakub, Nigeria

Twitter.com/emiinaa_h

A medical student in Oman, Amina Hussain El-Yakub is a Nigerian poet with recorded pieces of poetry and performance online.

Debbie Johnson, USA

TheDisabilityExperience.vpweb.com

With nearly 200 poems published in literary journals and anthologies including Ribbons, Prune Juice, Atlas Poetica, Page and Spine and several Lost Tower Anthologies, Debbie Johnson, particularly enjoys writing the Japanese forms. She is disabled and has done several poetry readings pertaining to disability. Her books include, The Disability Experience, The Disability Experience II, and Debbie's Friends, a book for children about disabilities.

Usha Krishnamurthy R., Bangalore, India
m.facebook.com/usha.krishnamurthy.568

A Lecturer in Business Law and also a Director for Textiles & Garment Procurement at Handikrafts Sourcing (exporters & importers of handicraft products, textiles, garments & handcrafted items, Usha Krishnamurthy, has been writing poetry since 1983. Many of her poems have been published in publications like "the Young Poets", "Poets International", "The Quest", "The World Poetry," etc. Usha's poems have been featured three times in the book "World Poetry" along with 150 poets. Those poems were "Symphony", "Search", and "A Letter." Her poems have been appreciated by Ms. Teresinka Pereira, USA, IWA, a Professor of Languages at Bluffton; Dr. Krishna Srinivas of World Poetry Society, Chennai (Founder-President and Editor-in-chief); the poet, Mr. Dwarkanath.H. Kabadi and many others. Usha's poems are borne out of real life situations, be they tragic, sentiments, love, humour, celebrations etc. She also writes personalised poems as per clients request for gifting purpose. The poem "My Parents" is dedicated to my parents who shaped my life into what I am today. It's an Ode to them. She is also a painter of murals, glass, oil, and water colours and a Beauty therapist.

Alicja Maria Kuberska, Inowroclaw, Poland

Facebook.com/alicja.kuberska.7

A novelist, journalist, editor, awarded Polish poetess, and member of the Polish Writers Associations in Warsaw, Alicja Maria Kuberska was born in 1960, in Świebodzin, Poland. In 2011 she published her first volume of poems entitled: "The Glass Reality." Her second volume "Analysis of Feelings", was published the following year followed by a third collection "Moments" published in English in 2014. That year she also published the novel - "Virtual roses" - and volume of poems "On the border of dream". Her "Girl in the Mirror" was published in the UK in 2015 and two volumes were published in the USA – "Love me" and "(Not) my poem." Recently she edited two anthologies "The Other Side of the Screen" and "Taste of Love."

Vimbai Josephine Lole, Harare, Zimbabwe

Embrace263.co.zw

A Zimbabwe poet, Vimbai Josephine Lole writes poetry for Zimlink and Reader's Cafe Africa.

Her poem for Zimbabwe Unity Day placed second in the 2010 national competition.

Glenna Luschei, Translator

Cathrine (Cat) Chidawanyika Makuvise, Zimbabwe

Kalabashmedia.com
Facebook.com/cathrine.chidawanyika

Cathrine is of the nomads and looks forward to exploring the world. Her spirit animal is an ever changing number of cats, sometimes she mewls, sometimes she roars. Having grown up with her voice in her throat, she found wings in words and became a word catcher. Cathrine is a Virgo, which is another way of saying awesome with a whole lot hidden crazy. She is a bush walker, beach lover, music addict who sings everywhere but the shower (sometimes silently), free spirit, cuddler, swearer. She does not believe the world is a stage and urges you to stop acting and start being.

Chiwawa Fungai (Leeyone) Manana, Zimbabwe

A lifelong song writer and poet, Chiwawa Fungai (Leeyone) Manana lives in Algeria.

Tanyaradzwa (Ty'ra Vanadis) Masaire, Zimbabwe

Vanadis17.wordpress.com
Facebook.com/vanadis.17

A poet and writer since age nine, Tanyaradzwa Masaire has a number of pieces published on her blog and various online media. She has written for Newsday and has performed at various events like the Black History Months hosted by Poets for Human Rights as well as the Book Café open mic sessions, Indab book café Poetry on Thursdays, Umlomo wakho Poetry sessions. One of Tanyaradzwa poems was included in one of the first anthologies curated by Thuthukani Ndlovu.

Kearoma Desiree (Mido) Mosata, Botswana

StrugglingBookworm.wordpress.com
Artsandafrica.com

A Motswana writer, feminist and sometimes a pretty decent spoken word poet, Kearoma Desiree Mosata, has hopes of one day packing everything up and living her life travelling and writing. She is an insatiable bookworm, a feminist and all round lover of all things involving art and African literature.

Xolani (X) Msimango, Bloemfontein, Free State, South Africa

ReintroductionOfMe.tumblr.com

My mirror is my stage, says Xolani Msimango, a South Africa law student. "I have never really been much of a performer, I've only ever performed on a proper stage twice. This right here is me making my merry way from behind the curtains into the spotlight."

Cheryl Zvikomborero Musimwa, Zimbabwe

HerMindinWords.wordpress.com

Facebook.com/cheryl.musimwa

This is Cheryl Zvikomborero Musimwa's first foray in world of published poets. Her work also exists on her blog. She performs regularly for the Wits Poets Corner, a university campus society that showcases poets and artists, about twice every semester. She is in her final year of law school.

Xeshelihle R. Ncube, Translator

Silindile Ndlovu, Translator

Thuthukani Ndlovu, Bloemfontein, South Africa

Radioactivetuts.blogspot.com/

Originally from Zimbabwe, Thuthukani Ndlovu is the curator of this collection of poetry. Thuthukani is a poet who not only writes, but also performs his poetry and enjoys creating platforms for poets to showcase their work. From anthologies to Open mic events, he seeks to encourage and inspire poets to write more, perform more, and develop their talents. A social activist and Christian, Thuthukani believes that poetry is powerful tool that can bring about social change. He likes to encourage people in the Arts and Entertainment industry to play an effective role in community development, as they tend to have a lot of influence on the general public.

Patience (Nana Ama) Osei Bonsu, Accra, Ghana

Poemhunter.com/nana-ama-emerald-osei-bonsu/

A teacher, Patience Osei Bonsu has published five poems on Poemhunter.com and various poetry communities. She also performs her poetry in her local Assemblies of God church.

Sandhya Padmanabhan, Bangalore, India

An assistant professor in Bangalore, India, Sandhya Padmanabhan was included in Best Poets 2015, the anniversary edition of Poets International.

Her poems have been published in the monthly journal brought out by Poets International. She is fascinated by the Japanese form of poetry, Haiku and has created close to 250 haiku for a forthcoming book.

Toiwa (P. A. Tunechi) Petronella, Pumula South, Bulawayo, Zimbabwe

As a "we the future "member, Toiwa (P. A. Tunechi) Petronella performs a poem under HYDT on world peace day at a road show held in Nkulumane (Sokusile).

Nyakallo (Azanian_Nile_Lily) Posholi, South Africa

Facebook.com/nyakallo.posholi1

An aspiring performing poet, Nyakallo Posholi has partaken in open mics around her home in Bloemfontein Free State (BFS) and in Qwa-qwa. She has been a poet from an early age when only a paper could understand and take her emotions. She is currently a child and youth development student.

Michelle L. Schmid, Rochester, MN, USA

A Communications and Collections Coordinator for Gagnon Art Museum in Rochester, MN, Michelle L. Schmid studied Creative Writing and poetry at the University of Wisconsin-Madison, contributed poetry to the Post Bulletin newspaper, and contributed poetry to Creative Communications Poetry Anthology for young writers for three years.

Linda Simone, San Antonio, TX, USA

LindaSimone.com
Twitter.com/lindsim1

Linda Simone's most recent chapbook is *Archeology* (Flutter Press, 2014). Her poems have appeared in more than 80 journals and 20 anthologies, and are forthcoming in anthologies about southwest personas and dogs. Her work is part of San Antonio Poet Laureate Laurie Ann Guererro's Love Poems to San Antonio installation, and VIA's Poetry on the Move poems on public transportation. A NY native, she now lives in San Antonio, Texas.

Itzel Adriana Sosa-Sánchez, Mexico

Laotrarevista.com/2012/03/itzela-sosa/

Born in Cuernavaca, Morelos Mexico, Itzela Sosa is a poet, translator and social researcher. She has published two poetry books: 'Open Sky Memories' (2009) and 'Stays' (2010). She has collaborated with several literary magazines in the state of Morelos and has been a member of the editorial board of different literary magazines and cultural news papers, among them Mala Vida and El Ojo, Correo Postal. Her poems have been included in several literary reviews and poetry anthologies in Mexico, Argentina, France-Québec, Peru, Colombia, Canada, España, Ecuador, and Estados Unidos (USA). In 2009, she was awarded the Hector de Saint-Denys Garneau Bourse-Prix (Québec, Canada) in the area of best literary creation with 'Tonale pour une nuit.' In 2008 her unpublished poetry book was awarded Best Literary Unpublished Book of the Year by the Institute of Culture of the State of Morelos. She has participated in several poetry events in Mexico and Latin America. Her poems have been translated and published in French, English, Catalan and Portuguese.

Rutendo Matewu (Heiressru) Tigere, Harare, Zimbabwe

Inferancesofanheiress.wordpress.com

Of her poetry experience, Rutendo Matewu Tigere says, "I have been writing poetry for as long as I can remember, each time I am inspired by something, or go through something my immediate response is to put pen to paper. I've never been much of a public speaker so I am yet to perform any of my poetry."

Latha. Y, Bangalore, India

A Librarian and teacher by profession, Latha Y has composed Free Verses and is very much interested in Japanese Classical poetic forms. She has composed Haiku, Renku, Zen, Haibun and other forms and will shortly be bringing out a book on Renku Poetry.

Ruth (Anastasia Ruth) Yacim, Nigeria

Anastasiaruth.wordpress.com

Poetry began for Ruth Yacim in school, where she was a member of Babcock University Literary Art Society (BULAS) during her undergraduate years; it is a creative society that promotes poetry and other forms literary art work. Ruth had her poems read and criticised and has since then had a book published "my naive collection". Of the collection she says, "It is as the name is - a collection of my early works which shows my early error and gradual growth in the world of poetry."

Index

Printed in Great Britain
by Amazon